Pirates

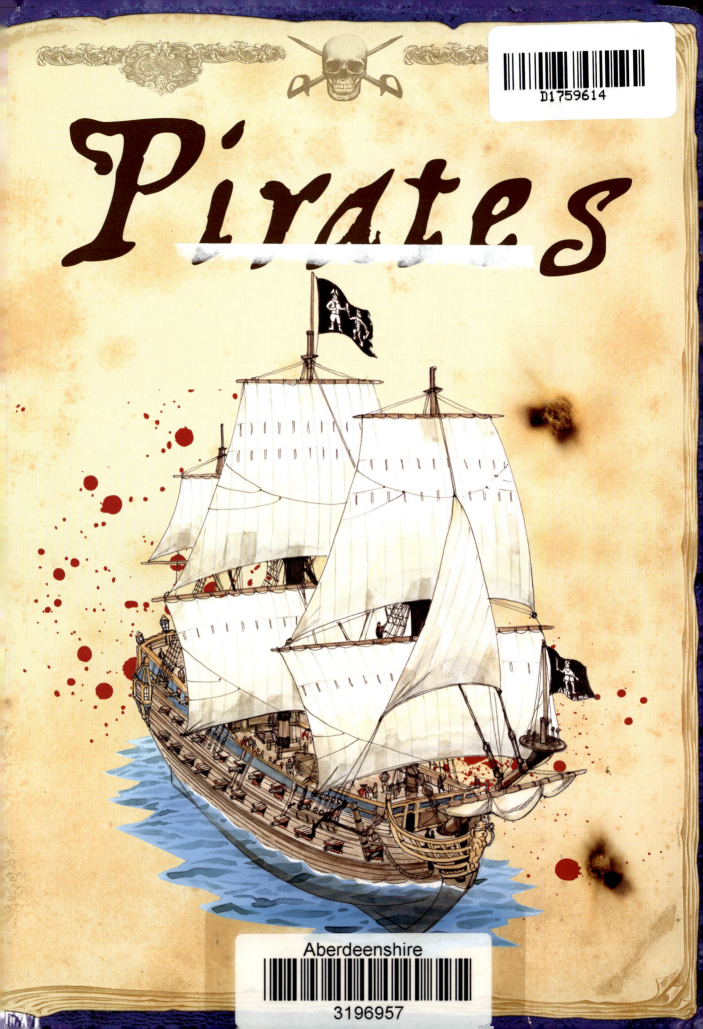

Contents

Published in Great Britain in MMXVI by
Book House, an imprint of
The Salariya Book Company Ltd
25 Marlborough Place, Brighton BN1 1UB
www.salariya.com

SALARIYA

135798642

A CIP catalogue record for this book is available
from the British Library.

Printed and bound in China.
Printed on paper from sustainable sources.

PB ISBN-13: 978-1-910706-74-9

Created and designed by: David Salariya
Additional illustrators: David Antram, John James
Editor: Jacqueline Ford

Visit
www.salariya.com
for our online catalogue and
fun **free** stuff.

PAPER FROM
SUSTAINABLE
FORESTS

Pirates

Nick Pierce

Illustrated by Mark Bergin

BOOK HOUSE
a SALARIYA imprint

A World of Pirates

Ever since ships first sailed, pirates have attacked them. Pirate raids on ancient Egypt were reported almost 4,000 years ago. Greek and Roman pirates seized ships and passengers, Vikings looted Europe and Chinese gangs terrorised Asian seas. These early pirates set a pattern of robbery with violence that continues today.

Blackbeard's Journal

"Pirates like myself have been feared by many for centuries. But we're not the simple devils our enemies would make us out to be. Many of us turned to piracy out of desperation or necessity. Of course, there is glory and wealth to be won as a pirate, but this is only half the story. I've decided to record this journal to give an insight into the triumphs and the hardships of a pirate's life. So, dear reader, if you wish to learn more, proceed..."

The Oxford, pirate Henry Morgan's flagship, blew up in the West Indies in 1669.

One of the richest treasure ships from the East, Las Chagas, was sunk by English pirates in 1594.

Henry Morgan sank the Magdalena in 1669 and salvaged the coins it was carrying.

English pirates captured the Rosario as it sailed to Panama in 1681. They thought its cargo was tin, and left it on board. But the 'tin' was really silver!

NORTH AMERICA

SOUTH AMERICA

SOUTH ATLANTIC OCEAN

Chinese pirates sailed in converted junks (cargo vessels). Their speed, cannons and big holds for storing gunpowder made them perfect for fighting. For hand-to-hand fighting, they favoured long, heavy swords that could slice through metal.

Barbary pirates lived on the southern shores of the Mediterranean and preyed on ships close to their home. They sailed in galleys – warships rowed by slaves who were whipped to make them go faster – and carried troops of janissaries (trained soldiers), ready to leap onto enemy ships and overpower the crew.

AFRICA

ASIA

SOUTH CHINA SEA

The Speaker, pirate John Bowen's ship, sank off Mauritius in 1702. Survivors paid the island's governor 2,100 pieces of eight to go free.

In 1407 the Chinese explorer Cheng Ho sank the ship of Ch'en Tsu-i when he attacked a fleet off the Sumatran coast.

Blackbeard's Journal

"Pirates are a motley, strange bunch, drawn from all nations and all walks of life. Some of us, like Francis Drake, have enjoyed fame and been loved by the public. Others toil away unnoticed aboard filthy ships, never amounting to anything. For my part, it has always been my ambition to become feared and respected..."

Buccaneers

Many buccaneers operated originally as privateers – private captains encouraged by governments to attack and raid enemy ships. In the 1500s, this was a cheap way for European countries to fight a war. In 1603, King James I of England banned privateering in the Caribbean.

Privateers in Hispaniola (present-day Haiti) formed gangs of lawless buccaneers in response to this. They were joined by escaped slaves and criminals. The buccaneers were ruthless pirates who terrorised the Spanish Main.

Map of Hispaniola

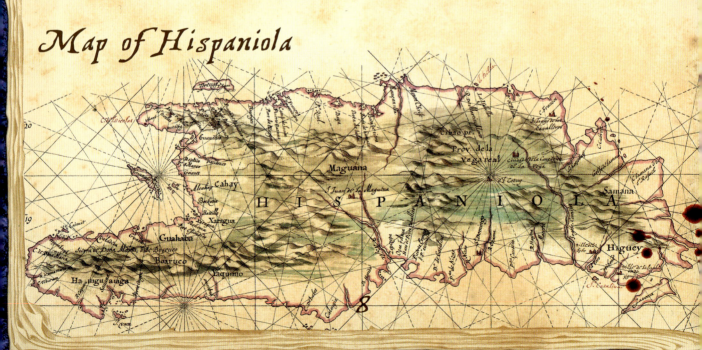

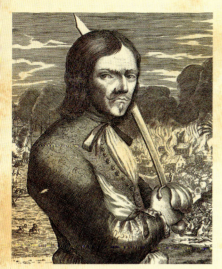

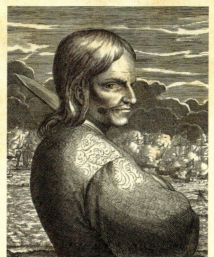

Bartholomew Roberts was a successful Welsh pirate who was killed during an attack in 1722. In two years he captured 400 ships, winning 'pleasure, liberty and power'.

Francois L'Olonnais arrived in the Caribbean as a servant, but made his name as a pirate who robbed ships from the Spanish West Indies and Spanish Main. He was notorious for torturing and violently killing his captives.

Roche Braziliano was a Dutch privateer who led a mutiny and became a bloodthirsty outlaw. He gained a reputation for shooting anyone who refused to drink with him. In 1671 he disappeared, his final fate unknown to this day.

Blackbeard

Edward Teach, born in Bristol, is much better known to us today by his pirate name of Blackbeard. His cruel ways and strange appearance, as presented by his first biographer Captain Charles Johnson in 1724, made him into a legend. According to Johnson, whose account of Blackbeard was probably highly fanciful, the pirate was covered in pistols and daggers and shot his own crew on a whim. However, it is more likely that Blackbeard used fear rather than violence to get his way. He was said to terrify the crews on ships he plundered by tying lit fuses under his hat before boarding them.

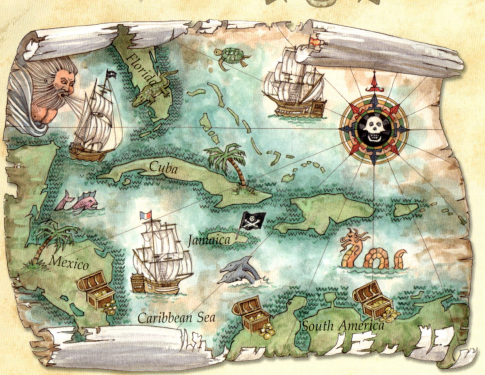

1716: The Caribbean Sea is the haunt of English Pirates. These rogues are the menace of the Spanish Main. The pirates lie in wait for Spanish treasure ships full of valuables plundered from the peoples of the New World.

The Spanish Main

The Spanish Main was the name given to the area that stretches from the north coast of South America to Florida in North America. The name came from the fact that there were many Spanish settlements in the seas around South America. Pirates and privateers from many European countries prowled these waters, eager to attack Spanish treasure ships.

Blackbeard's Journal

"These days, I mainly call the Spanish Main my home, although I also travel along the eastern coast of the American colonies. These waters offer rich pickings for unwary and defenceless treasure ships. If a pirate is capable, smart and lucky, he can avoid capture and become wealthy by preying on such vessels..."

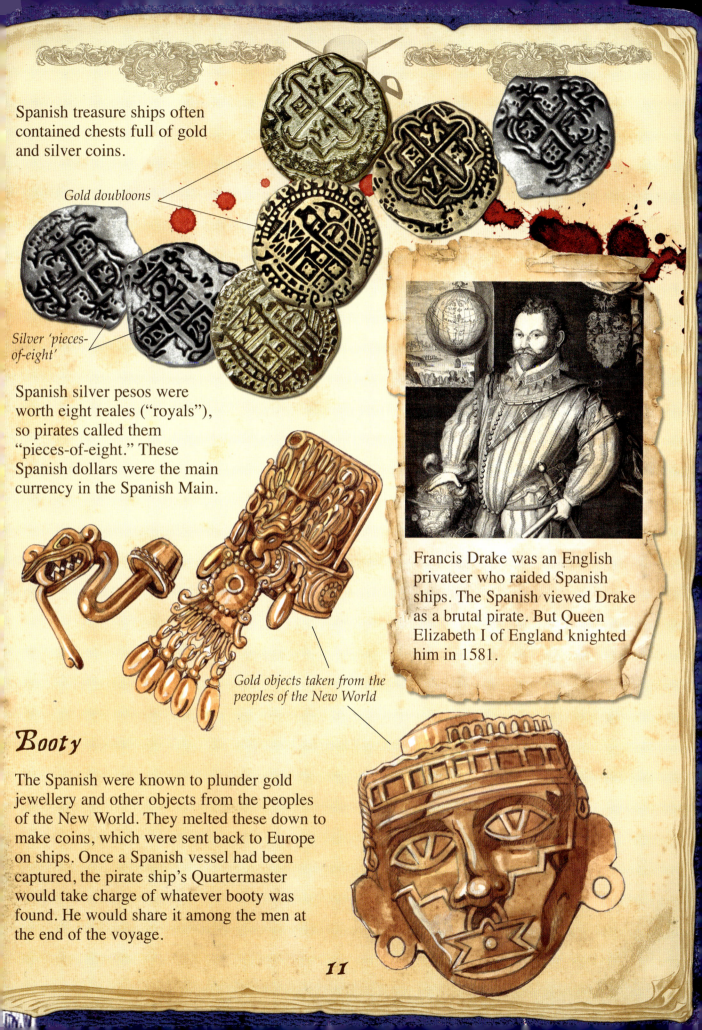

Spanish treasure ships often contained chests full of gold and silver coins.

Gold doubloons

Silver 'pieces-of-eight'

Spanish silver pesos were worth eight reales ("royals"), so pirates called them "pieces-of-eight." These Spanish dollars were the main currency in the Spanish Main.

Francis Drake was an English privateer who raided Spanish ships. The Spanish viewed Drake as a brutal pirate. But Queen Elizabeth I of England knighted him in 1581.

Gold objects taken from the peoples of the New World

Booty

The Spanish were known to plunder gold jewellery and other objects from the peoples of the New World. They melted these down to make coins, which were sent back to Europe on ships. Once a Spanish vessel had been captured, the pirate ship's Quartermaster would take charge of whatever booty was found. He would share it among the men at the end of the voyage.

Pirate Port

The wild, lawless Jamaican town of Port Royal was the home port for many pirate ships of the Spanish Main. The town had many wealthy merchants who would buy any looted gold, silver and jewellery cheaply. They sold it in London for a high price, and with their profits they bought supplies of food and other goods to sell to pirates in Port Royal.

Blackbeard's Journal

"When we're not at sea, my crew and I like to relax on shore in places like Port Royal. You'll be made welcome in the port's taverns. But a word of caution. These places are the hangouts of thieves and tricksters who will try to separate you from your money..."

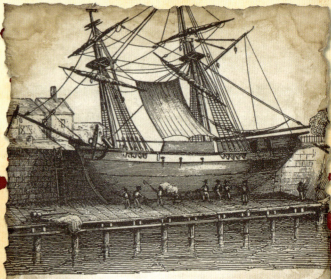

Wooden ships required caulking. Cotton or hemp fibres, soaked in tar, were driven between planks to make ships watertight.

Pirate ships

W
hat did a pirate ship like Blackbeard's look like and how was it organised?

The bow

The bow or forward section of a ship was where the crew lived on board. 'Forecastle' or 'fo'c'sl hands' remained a familiar term for a ship's crew throughout the age of sail.

The stern

The most comfortable area of a ship lay aft of the waist (the ship's centre section). It was here in the stern that the ship's captain had his cramped cabins and the ship was steered.

All the ship's provisions were stored near the galley, where the food was prepared. Fire aboard ship was a constant danger, and the galley fire was only lit for short periods when the sea was not too rough.

Queen Anne's Revenge, 1718

Rigging

Fore course

Bowsprit

Spritsail

Bow

The rigging

The long ocean voyages made during the 16th century led to great changes in the rigging of ships. On such voyages there were always many deaths from sickness, accidents or battle. More and more block-and-pulley tackles were used as labour-saving devices. These made it possible for the reduced crew to sail the ship home.

The slave trade

For voyages across the Atlantic Ocean, slaves were chained below decks with little food or water. Thousands of them died. Survivors were sold at public auction.

West Indies
North America
Britain
West Africa

Atlantic slave trade triangle

Between 1500 and 1800, about 12 million slaves were shipped from Africa to the Americas.

The slave trade triangle transported guns and cloth to Africa and sugar back to Europe.

Sugar beet

Sugar root

Plantations

Millions of African slaves were worked to death in appalling conditions on the plantations of the New World. No wonder many escaped slaves were happy to join pirate gangs!

The Capture of the Revenge

A treasure ship being pursued by the pirates

Fore topgallant sail

Fore topsail

Jib

Bowsprit

Spritsail

Fore course

Bow

Blackbeard's famous vessel was originally a French slave ship called *La Concorde* transporting its human cargo across the Caribbean. The ship surrendered to Blackbeard after being pursued by him.

Captain and Crew

Canvas rags, smeared in black tar to protect from the cold and wet.

Cocked hat with a feather

Silk sash

*T*he Captain expected every seaman to know his place and do his duty the best he could. In return for hard work and loyalty, the crew received a share of any treasure taken. The size of the share depended on the job they did.

The Captain was the ship's commander. He gave orders during battle. He was voted captain because the crew looked up to him as a strong leader.

Blackbeard's Journal

"There are many reports of my so-called barbaric behaviour, but these are largely false. I prefer to command respect among my crew and prisoners by appearing fierce and powerful, rather than by using violence..."

16

Mizzen sail

Blackbeard's flag

Ship's deck

Stern

'Great Cabin'
for captain

Lower or orlop deck

Ballast in bilge

The Making of a Ship

Ships were built in shipyards. A busy shipyard gave regular employment to scores of people: craftsmen, boy apprentices learning their trade, and suppliers of raw materials.

Pitch-heaters prepared tar for waterproofing plank seams.

Carpenter and joiner.

Blacksmiths' forges provided ironwork

Mastmakers at work planing off the angles to make a new mast.

Trenail mooters fixed planking with wooden pins called trenails.

The suppliers were hardly less important than the craftsmen working on the ships. They provided everything from timber to hemp for ropes and cables, iron for the nailmakers, smith and coopers, and pitch for the caulkers.

Many of these materials had to be brought from overseas and supplying them to the yards was an important trade in itself. Shipyard workers also had constant work repairing and rebuilding existing ships.

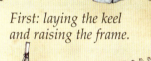
First: laying the keel and raising the frame.

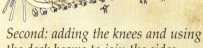
Second: adding the knees and using the deck beams to join the sides.

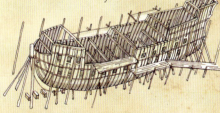

Third: Completing the side planking and cutting square ports for the guns.

The sailmaker cut and stitched the sails.

A caulker sealed planking seams with greased rope.

Riggers prepared the ropes and rigging. Blockmakers made the pulleys and heavy blocks needed to raise and lower the sails.

Fourth: The new galleon is ready to launch. The seams are caulked and the scaffolding taken down.

Main topsail

Mizzen topsail

Mizzen sail

Pirate flag

Stern

Main course

Deck

Rigging

Blackbeard had the ship altered to fit his requirements. His crew cut extra gun ports and removed the forecastle and quarterdeck. When it was finished, the ship had 40 guns and was even more powerful than most of the local warships. Blackbeard renamed it *Queen Anne's Revenge*.

Flintlock pistol

Leather strap for
holding weapons

Bandana

Silver-buckled shoes

If the Captain showed
weakness at sea, the crew
could choose another
man as captain. The
Quartermaster was second
in command and would
take charge of the rations
and captured booty. He
was the only man allowed
to whip a seaman.

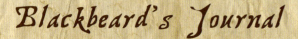

Blackbeard's Journal

"Being able to successfully plunder a ship is only half a pirate's job. If you don't have crew members who can navigate, you're doomed to run your vessel aground or become hopelessly lost..."

Wrecks

Ships that failed to navigate well by paying attention to their surroundings were in danger of drifting into hazardous waters and being dashed to pieces on rocks.

Navigation

The navigator used the best scientific equipment available to find the ship's position at sea. In the daytime he took bearings based on the height of the sun in relation to the horizon. At night, the moon and stars helped him to fix the ship's course.

Hourglasses

Compass and hourglass

A compass was used to find out which direction was which so that the navigator could plot a course accordingly. Hourglasses were used to measure the time a route was taking. This helped to determine whether the ship was still on course.

Compass

Cross-staff

A cross-staff was used to measure angles, such as the angle between the horizon and the Sun. This helped to measure distances.

Backstaff

By using a backstaff the navigator could calculate the ship's position. To use a backstaff, stand with your back to the midday sun, hold the staff straight and look along it to the horizon. Note the angle of the shadow, from which you can work out the ship's position, called latitude.

Astrolabe

This device could be used to locate the stars, Sun, Moon and planets, aiding navigation.

Maps

You did not disturb the Captain as he studied his charts. At the same time each day the navigator worked out the ship's position, which the Captain plotted on a chart. With his dividers he measured the distance sailed from day to day, and checked that all was well with the course.

Map

Pirate Weapons

Once the pirates had taken over a ship, seamen who resisted would come face to face with any of the vast amount of weapons the pirates held. In hand-to-hand fighting, they used axes, swords, daggers and pikes to cut through their enemies' tough leather clothes and pierce the skin.

Grenades were lit and thrown at enemies, exploding and flinging lead shot in every direction.

Weapons

Pirates used flintlock muskets for shooting at a distance and flintlock pistols for close combat. Both shot heavy balls of lead.

Cannons

Pirate ships often carried small cannons to intimidate the enemy. It took at least three men to operate a cannon, firing one iron cannonball every ten minutes over a distance of about 150 metres (492 feet).

Pirate tactics

In most battles, surprise was the best tactic. Ships waited until the last moment to raise their flag. Their victims wouldn't know it was an enemy ship until too late.

If you were asked to make a Jolly Roger, the captain would tell you what design he wanted. The bolder the design, the more it would frighten your enemy.

Private warships called "privateers", which were given permission by their governments to plunder enemy ships, flew the flags of their countries.

Pirate flags

The skull and crossbones on pirate flags were symbols understood by seamen of all nations. They stood for death and violence. Many prize ships surrendered when they saw them.

The skull and crossbones

John Rackham's flag

Blackbeard's flag

Henry Every's flag

Bartholomew Roberts' two flags.

Earrings

Superstitious pirates thought that wearing earrings improved poor eyesight and protected the wearer from harm!

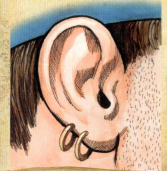

Smoke signals

Pirates sometimes used fires on shore to send messages to ships at sea. They would hold material over the smoke to alternate the rate at which it rose into the air.

Food and Drink

A pirate ship carried enough food and drink to last at least until it reached a port to refresh its supplies. Fresh food didn't last long and even dry food turned bad in the damp air of the ship's hold. Only heavily salted fish and meat lasted the length of long trips. Strongly flavoured drinks helped to wash the meals down.

A pirate's menu

Ships sailed with live hens, which provided fresh meat and eggs. Fresh fish could be caught from the sea too, but on days when there was no fresh food, pirates had to chew on ship's biscuits. These were known as "hardtack" because they were so tough. Pirates couldn't complain if they found a maggot in them (they ate the biscuits, too).

Blackbeard's journal

"A pirate crew sails on its stomach! Without enough food and drink to go around, your crew won't have the strength or the will to capture other ships. If things get too bad, they might even rise up and replace the captain.

Of course, the food on offer isn't always the finest. After a long time at sea, the supplies can become basic and mouldy. Sometimes, if you're not careful, the rats and maggots can get at the food before you do..."

Scurvy

There weren't many fresh fruits or vegetables on ships. This posed a risk of scurvy – a disease caused by lack of Vitamin C. The symptoms include: blotches and sores on the skin, pimples on the gums, teeth falling out and feeling weak.

Vitamin C is found in citrus fruits like lemons

Fresh water turned foul on long voyages, so the ship carried bottles of ale for the crew to drink.

Pirates took a daily swig of "Rumbullion", a sweet alcohol made from molasses. The English called it "rum".

Wine

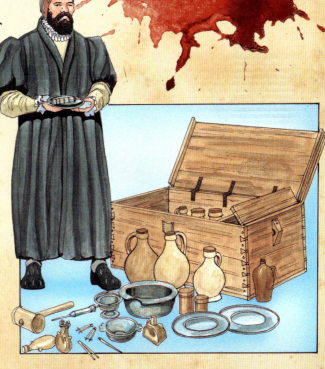

Before drinking wine, a pirate would check that the cork was well tied on or else the contents could be sour.

Ships usually carried a medical doctor known as a barber-surgeon. His equipment would include jars of ointment, drug flasks, syringes, bowls and a mallet for knocking out a patient before an operation.

Pirates of the Caribbean

Cocked hat with feathers

Leather strap for holding weapons

Velvet jacket

Blackbeard was not the only pirate operating in the Caribbean to make a name for himself. There are many other buccaneers from the period whose criminal careers have passed into legend. Altogether, and with the help of fictional stories inspired by them, they have formed our romantic, appealing view of the pirates of the Caribbean.

Trousers tied at the knee

Stockings

Henry Morgan

Sir Henry Morgan was a Welsh pirate who raided cities in Central America and the Caribbean in the 1660s. He went to the Spanish Main when he was young, wanting to win fame and fortune by fighting against Spain. He led shiploads of savage buccaneers on secret English missions to attack Spanish settlements. In 1671, he destroyed Panama, a peaceful Spanish city, and was sent home in disgrace. He was pardoned, however, because England needed his skills and knowledge.

Silver-buckled shoes

Edward Low

A cruel English pirate. He killed 53 Spanish captives with his cutlass, and he burnt a French cook alive, saying he was "a greasy fellow who would fry well". Low was captured and hanged in 1723.

Black Bart

He liked fine clothes and drank tea. He was a good sailor and a brave fighter. His crew of 254 included 70 African slaves.

Women pirates

Anne Bonny became a pirate on John Rackham's ship alongside Mary Read, but they had to dress as men to hide their identities – women were not allowed on pirate ships as they were thought to bring bad luck. During a raid along the north coast of Jamaica in 1720, Rackham's ship was seized. Whilst the men were hanged, the women were spared as they were pregnant.

Blackbeard's Journal

"Great news! Today we managed to board a merchant ship. The crew, terrified by our speed, firepower and fearsome appearances, surrendered almost at once..."

Sea Battles

Smoke and screams would fill the air as a pirate ship drew alongside its victim, a slow Spanish merchant ship. Cannons and bombs exploded, and muskets were fired. The raiders pulled the ship closer with grappling hooks and slashed its ropes to bring down the sails.

27

Terror

Pirates would prepare to board a ship by yelling threats and waving their weapons in the air.

Surrender

Full-blown battles were very rare. Pirates usually laid traps or used scare tactics. Captains knew that if they lost a fight, the pirates' revenge would be horrific. Most surrendered quietly.

A Grim Punishment

Captured pirates faced very harsh punishments for their crimes. These were designed to act as a warning to others, showing them that the reward for a life of piracy was to meet a nasty, painful or humiliating end. However, few pirates were ever brought to trial. Most died at sea or lived to enjoy their booty.

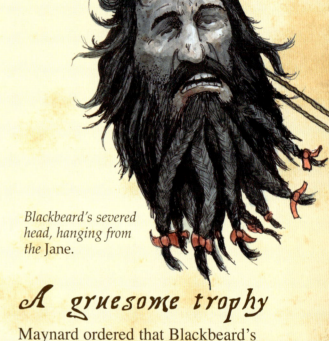

Blackbeard's severed head, hanging from the Jane.

Blackbeard's end

On 22nd November 1718, Blackbeard's well-armed vessel the *Adventure* was pursued by Lieutenant Robert Maynard of the Royal Navy. Maynard cleverly hid most of his crew below decks, so that Blackbeard believed his enemy were outnumbered.

Blackbeard decided to board Maynard's ship, only to find the lieutenant's men surging up onto the deck as he did so. In the following fight, Blackbeard was killed.

A gruesome trophy

Maynard ordered that Blackbeard's decapitated head be hung from the bowsprit of his sloop, the *Jane*.

Captured pirates had their legs clamped in large, heavy irons called bilboes. They remained fastened to the deck until brought to shore to face justice.

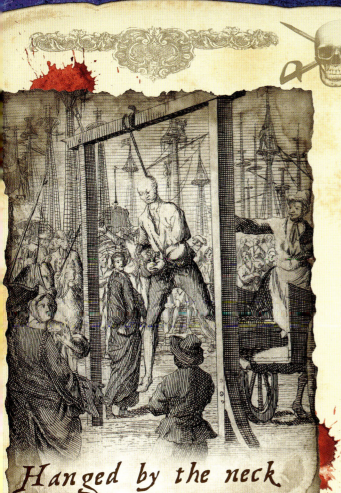

Put on display

Before hanging, a pirate was measured for a steel cage where his dead body would be displayed. This way, it would still look human as it rotted. Sometimes it was coated in tar to make it rot even more slowly. The remains were placed at the water's edge as a warning to others. The cage stopped relatives cutting down the body and burying it.

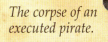

Hanged by the neck

This was the punishment for convicted pirates. Audiences were encouraged to watch. The corpse was strung from a wooden frame called a gibbet.

The corpse of an executed pirate.

The hulks

Pirates lucky enough to escape hanging were often sent to prison hulks. These were ships that housed prisoners. Hulks were cold, damp and crawling with rats and lice.

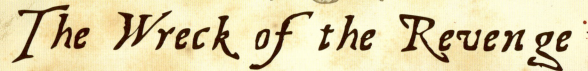

The Wreck of the Revenge

Despite the ship's fame, *Queen Anne's Revenge* was only used by Blackbeard for a year before he ran it aground at Beaufort Inlet in North Carolina in 1718.

Map of the wreck site near Beaufort Inlet, North Carolina.

An illustration of Queen Anne's Revenge *at sea before it was run aground.*

In 1996, a private research firm discovered the wreck of the *Revenge* off the coast of North Carolina and began salvaging artifacts from it.

A research vessel

The wreck of Queen Anne's Revenge

Cast iron swivel gun

Crucifix

Cast iron grenade

Perfume pitcher

Pestle and mortar

Weight used to measure coinage

Syringe

Silver coins

Ship's bell

Various pieces of equipment and valuables have been recovered from the wreck, although much more still lies on the seabed. Among the objects are more than thirty cannons of different sizes. They come from different European countries, and seem to have been cobbled together into one arsenal by the pirate crew. Personal belongings such as buttons, counters from a game, and the fragments of a pipe have also been collected.

33

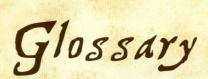

Glossary

Astrolabe Instrument for finding the altitude of the sun or a star, to fix the ship's latitude.

Booty Goods stolen on a pirate raid.

Bow The front of a ship.

Bowsprit Spar extending from the bow to brace the fore-topmast and carry a spritsail.

Cross-staff A navigation instrument for finding latitude.

Cutlass Short sword, often with a curved blade.

Doubloon Spanish gold coin.

Fo'c'sl (pronounced 'FOAK-sull') Sailor's pronunciation of 'forecastle'.

Gibbet Wooden frame for hanging a pirate's corpse.

Jolly Roger Pirate flag, usually red or black and decorated with skulls, crossbones, and swords. Each pirate had his own design.

Junk Chinese sailing ship, made of wood with a flat bottom and square sails.

Lateen A triangular sail supported by a slanting yard.

New World Name given to the Americas after colonisation by Europeans in the 1500s.

Pirate Robber or other criminal of the seas.

Plunder To steal goods.

Privateer A type of pirate ship whose crew works for a government.

Shot Small lead pellets used in shotguns.

Spanish Main Spanish colonies in the Americas, stretching from Panama to the Orinoco River and including the Caribbean Sea.

Spritsail Square sail attached to a yard hung from the bowsprit.

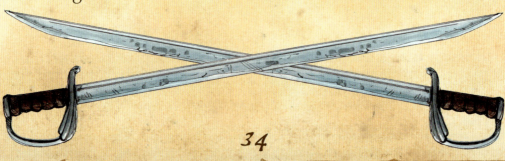

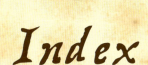

Index